The Gentle Man

Also by Bart Edelman

Crossing the Hackensack
Under Damaris' Dress
The Alphabet of Love

⇥ BART EDELMAN ⇤

The Gentle Man

poems

Red Hen Press Los Angeles 2001

The Gentle Man
Copyright © 2001 by Bart Edelman

All rights reserved.

No part of this book may be used or reproduced in any manner whatever without written permission except in the case of brief quotations embodied in critical articles and reviews.

Acknowledgments: "Bashevis," "Forgiveness," "In Albany Love," and "Your Father's Ghost" first appeared in *Clackamas Literary Review*. "Photograph (circa 1960)" and "So Much Like Marie" first appeared in *Flint Hills Review*.

Special thanks to Susan Cisco, Mark Cull and Kate Gale.

Cover art: "Surf and Turf"
      by Ilana Bloch, Los Angeles, California

Author photograph: Jackie Houchin

Book and cover design: Mark E. Cull

First Edition
ISBN 1-888996-33-1
Library of Congress Catalog Card Number: 00-109764

Published by: Red Hen Press
              www.redhen.org

for all the little ghosts . . .

Table of Contents

The Gentle Man	11
Johnny	12
Broken Hearts	14
Bashevis	16
The Love Prayer	17
Baby Harold	18
Recipe	20
The Day the House Moved Away	21
Parker's Law	22
In Albany Love	23
TAPS	24
The Poet Speaks of Desire	26
Jersey Air	27
The Girl You Love to Hate	28
Photograph (circa 1960)	30
So Much Like Marie	31
What I Could Have Been	32
Forgiveness	33
The Chief	34
Five Blind Boys	36
Dream House	38
Winter's Night	39
Chemistry Experiment	40
Revelations	41
The Good Life	42
So What	45

Undone	46
Your Father's Ghost	47
This Case for You	48
U.S.A.	50
The Plaintive Angel	51
Timber	52
Nursery of Lies	54
Hair Care	55
Only a Game	56
Memorandum	58
Bats	59
Poetry (In Motion)	60
Doctors of Letters	62
The Locomotive to Hell	63
Dangerous Curve	64
Obituary	65
Love Story	66
The Cost of Being Me	68
70	70
Losing Olivia	72
Reaching for Heaven	73
Dwiggins	74
Last Request	76

The Gentle Man

The Gentle Man

In the tender hands
Of the gentle man,
Love grows like a rose
Whose petals open to show
The woman he knows.
And soft is his touch
That strokes her skin—
This slow, kind act
For which she wishes
To grant him forgiveness
The moment he asks it.
She wonders where he learned
The lost art of hesitation,
How kiss and caress differ
In every conceivable way
And why one of his glances
Makes her knees quiver.
Each night she prays
He will never go away,
Leaving her vacant and dry,
Unable to seize the desire
Which waits so patiently
In the tender hands
Of the gentle man.

Johnny

Between Spaulding and Stanley,
Somewhere off Sunset,
Johnny comes clean;
He tells me, matter of factly,
He's been living on rice and beans
For a few months now
And, frankly, he's sick of it all.
The roof over his head
Crashes down around him every night
And he thinks he may leave L.A.
"Nobody wants their photograph taken any more,"
He says, fingering the trusty Nikon
He married 25 years ago.
"I used to snap every one of 'em:
Ginsberg, Burroughs, Dylan and Ali.
Now I can't pay the guy down the block
To sit and stare into the lens.
I gotta get a Bar Mitzvah next week
Just to pay the damn rent.
Jesus Christ, I never pictured this."

Johnny does look a bit gaunt;
His hair is beginning to thin
And go gray around the temples.
He's a far cry from the guy
I knew back in Brooklyn,
When we were high school boys
Who often ducked into the Village
To listen to Mose or Earl.
"Can I give you a little something?"
I ask rather stupidly
Because I'm feeling lousy
And think he certainly doesn't deserve
The slap in the face
Fate delivers each day.
"Nah, I'll manage—I always do."

Then he points the camera at me
And steadies the shot.
Slowly releasing the shutter,
Johnny turns and whistles,
Winding his way towards Fountain.

Broken Hearts

He had not yet met
A damaged woman he didn't love.
They came to him
In all sizes and shapes,
And he kept them for months,
Attempting to mend each one
Before he sent them
Back on the street again.

Here were hungry women
Without names or faces—
Girls who couldn't quite guess
What to make of their lives;
Always watching and praying
For days which never arrived,
Nights that left nothing more
Than an empty circle of sleep.

So good did he eventually grow
At his collectable craft
That women stood in line
To plead each separate case.
There was much hand wringing
And the jerking of tears;
Soon he had to add
An extra story to his house.

The neighbors assumed he must be
Some type of petty criminal.
They filed countless complaints,
Alleging he was up to no good;
But that didn't stop him
From filling the floors
With waif-like waitresses
And an occasional obese usherette.

In the end, then,
His home became a hotel
Whose revolving doors opened
To women from around the world.
Here he worshipped a single truth
Behind four granite walls,
Where he lovingly exchanged
One broken heart for another.

Bashevis

In a strange tongue
They tell us is mute,
You spoke for those who now
Peddle their gabardine dreams
Six feet beneath the earth.

What Warsaw was then . . .
When Krochmalna Street bustled
With Jew after unsuspecting Jew,
You refused to surrender,
Long after the hateful race
Disfigured each face
And charred hope forever—
A layer of powdered ash.

A swank continent away,
On some unholy day,
You lit the only candle worth saving;
One tiny flame flickered
In a miserable heart.

To say the distant madness
Never touched you in America
Dismisses the dozen dibbuks,
Howling by your back door,
Dying to tear at your soul.

Ah, noble Bashevis—
Spinner of improbable yarns,
Mystical seeker of vision;
Where do you sleep tonight?
Your hairless head heavy,
Your pen poised and ready
To write the family name
Upon every dusty tomb of life.

—for Isaac Bashevis Singer

The Love Prayer

Often we speak of love
As if it were the only prayer,
Something to get us through the night
Or mark deliberate days
On the calendar we keep
In the soft cells of our brains.
There is the notion that love
Staves off whatever ravages
Life holds over each of us:
The idea that poverty is more bearable,
Hatred, in some way, almost tenable,
And sickness, entirely treatable,
If we quicken the beat
In the catacomb of the heart.
Perhaps, this is the reason
Clever clerics walk a thin line
Between petitioning God through grace,
Allowing passion its own reward.
And it's better left this way,
Where benevolent men and women
Profess silent vows of chastity—
Voices never raised above a whisper.

Baby Harold

Baby Harold is unhappy again;
They've been taunting him
At the elementary school
And he wants a new name.
He'd prefer to be called Lance
Or Logan or Barry or Bill—
Anything but Baby Harold!
We tell him every night
That he has a fine name
He'll grow into some day
If he's just patient enough.

Baby Harold closes his bedroom door
And states he won't come out.
He's stewing and we know what this means.
He'll pout and act surly
For a good part of the evening
And it won't be fun for anyone.
I wish he took after his sisters;
Everything rolls off their backs.
What's in a name, anyway?
When he reaches the age of 21,
He can change it if he chooses,
But I'll bet he'll be fond of it by then.

Baby Harold eventually decides
We're worthy of his presence
And strolls into the living room.
He sits on his mother's lap,
Wearing the Cincinnati Reds cap
I bought him this afternoon.
He says he wants to play baseball
And be just like Hal Morris.
When I tell him Hal's real name is Harold
He seems rather puzzled for a moment;
Then he suddenly becomes pleased,
Beaming as if he's just seen the light.

Somewhere around midnight
I check up on Baby Harold
And discover him asleep in bed,
A small bat in his hands.
I remove it very gently
And find his little fingers
Tightly grasping my own,
As if he's holding on for dear life.
Perhaps, he's dreaming of the big game,
Hearing the crowd scream out
The same name I've learned to love
Ever since I was a boy.

Recipe

I would like to think
This meal is now over—
That I have cooked
The last batch of sorrow;
Peeled, diced, grated and sliced,
Measured, seasoned, roasted and reasoned,
To my faint heart's content.
And I finally realize
Why this is a recipe
I am able to prepare,
But unwilling to serve.

In the kitchen of good fortune
I admit I stumbled badly.
Whatever flavors we craved,
Never reached the table
When company came calling,
Demanding the staged show.
And well-stocked as we appeared,
There was always one key ingredient
Amiss among the melange.

Perhaps, if it were only
A simple matter of choice,
Everything would be forgiven
And we could just try again;
After all, it takes time
To learn a new skill.
Yet this terrible taste
Lingers in my mouth,
And I suspect the thought of food
Will keep me hungry no more.

The Day the House Moved Away

The day the house moved away
We were far too numb
To say a single word
And shed a tear.
It was long overdue,
Like a library book
We'd simply forgotten about—
Or stashed in the trunk of our car.
But lying there in bed,
Listening to the walls lament,
Before they stumbled down the hallway
And out the front door,
Brought us closer to the truth.
I don't know when that old house
Realized we didn't care—
How lazy and complacent we'd grown.
And what would it have taken:
A fresh coat of paint?
New tiles for the floor?
Paintings to cover the bare walls?
Now, nothing but bricks and mortar
Spill into a river of rubble
Which flows past our toes.
Carelessly strewn clothes hang
Over enormous wooden chairs
That sit vacantly still,
Where we stretched ancient dreams
Across our tired little lives
And built this legacy of despair—
One room at a time.

Parker's Law

They call it Parker's Law
And name it after you—
This concept which states
If a body remains at rest
Too long in one location
It never leaves that place,
Because there's only so much land
To go around these days
And wherever it is you stand,
You really ought to stay put
And sit down for the duration.

They award you an honorary degree
And a senior faculty position
At the local community college
And all they ask is that you
Teach one course each semester,
Revealing the ins and outs
Of the enlightened state of inertia,
A rather new field of science
That's popular across the nation.

Many years later, when you find yourself
Extremely long in the tooth
And short in the saddle,
It occurs to you to admit
There has always been a fatal flaw
In the heart of your immutable law,
But you're far too tired now
To conduct the proper research
And return the medals of honor
They've strung around your neck.
Besides, any movement, whatsoever,
May well lead to paralysis—
The opiate of the dead.

In Albany Love

In Albany love
Taps me on the shoulder
And when I whirl around
There you stand, laughing,
Your suitcase packed,
A map in your hand.

In Albany love
Arrives in the middle of spring,
Floating on feathered wings,
Lighter than the breeze
That rolls off the Hudson—
And we catch it just right.

In Albany love
Drops softly from trees
And blankets the city streets
We walk hour after hour,
In search of a neighborhood
We can both call home.

In Albany love
Allows us to review
The course of history
It took to find us here,
Where we build a little house
On a lot outside Loudonville.

In Albany love
Teaches us how kindness
Is really hope in disguise,
How patience gets a bad rap,
And how nothing in this world
Will ever be the same again.

TAPS

I'd suffered more than enough
And decided to call it quits.
I got my affairs in order
And left no stone unturned.
I wasn't surprised, at all,
That it had come to this.
Death had been busy barking
Up the branches of my tree
For an awfully long time.

I'd always heard it said:
No man is an island.
Yet whoever spoke such words
Didn't know me in the least.
I never met a man I liked—
For even so much as a moment.
Will Rogers was nothing
But a great big liar
Who got kicked in the head
By one too many horses.

So I guess it's pretty well done.
I'm leaving whatever I have
To an old broad in Spokane;
She showed me a few good times
When I was down in the mouth
Over the damn V.A.'s failure
To pay me what I was owed
And get me the proper treatment
For a nagging neck injury
I've been nursing since 'Nam.

Ah, what's it all mean?
Now I just need to decide
How to do the dirty deed.
I got plenty of pain pills,
A gun, a knife, a syringe—
Even a plastic bag for the occasion—
And a hotel room on the top floor,
So high I can see the entire city.
Believe me, I won't be missed.
I guess I'd just like to hear
The sound of a bugle
Before I hit the street.

The Poet Speaks of Desire

The poet speaks of desire
And ten women swoon
Across a crowded room.
He is quite tired and bored
From the lengthy book tour
And wants nothing more
Than to crawl back home
To his life of familiarity—
Where wife, children and work
Consume his days and nights
And steady the ground
Where he walks each week.

The poet speaks of desire
And the chairs begin to tingle
Beneath the bottoms of women
Who had given up on love
Only a few hours ago.
He reads each particular poem
As if it were the first time
He let the words out of his sight
And wonders, in certain cases,
If they make any sense.

Much later that evening,
Under the cover of darkness,
Where private thoughts
Lead to public denials,
The women who intensely watch
The poet speak of desire,
Open up their secret lives
And dream of runaway brides
On horses so fast they actually fly—
While the poet, overtaken by sleep,
Dreams of endless research papers,
Leaky faucets and Little League games.

Jersey Air

On the side of Route 4,
Two skunks struck dumb
By a speeding Buick—
Hellbent on reaching home
Before the dinner bell rang.
How is it hope springs
Eternal in the human breast,
But no more in skunk brains
That litter the local highway
This hot summer night.
And of the pair,
One appeared tiny and frail;
The other—perhaps the mother?
May well have known
Their crossing was a bad idea,
But went on nonetheless
And tossed maternal instinct
Into an abysmal wind—
The smell of which lingers
Long past midnight
Through the thick Jersey air.

The Girl You Love to Hate

The girl you love to hate
Strides into the restaurant,
Confident and self-assured.
She's quite tall and lanky
With hair halfway down her back
And she's wearing no makeup.
The white cotton summer dress
She's selected for the afternoon
Clings to her tan skin and rests
Three inches above her knees.
There's a table already set for her
In the middle of the room—
And you wonder who will join her.

From the corner of your eye
You spy the girl you love to hate,
As her long delicate fingers
Grasp a glass of water
And raise it to curved lips
You swear must be collagen injected,
Although you know it's not the case;
But this is exactly what
You would tell your best friend
If she were there with you now—
And she would certainly agree.

One by one, heads turn
Towards the girl you love to hate.
Men, women and children
Measure her perfect face
And stillness fills the room.
A man enters the restaurant
In search of the girl who sighs
The moment she sees him
Drop into the chair beside her.

Soon his hand slips between hers,
The clatter of dishes resumes
And people regain the voices
They traded for beauty's silence.
Amid the afternoon glow
You lower your eyes
When you feel shame's stain
Crawl slowly over you.
But the vision of the girl
Refuses to vanish entirely—
And you realize, again,
Just how much you hate her.

Photograph (circa 1960)

You open the freezer one morning
In search of an onion bagel
To suppress last night's hunger
And find an old photograph
Hidden among the frozen foods.
You don't question how it got there—
Stranger things have happened;
Rather, you take it in stride
And begin the thawing process.
About an hour or two later
It all comes into focus:
The year is circa 1960,
Your family carefully posed
Around the backyard swimming pool
Which will one day swallow
Your younger brother, Herbert,
Who will lie, motionless,
At the bottom of the deep end,
Before he is discovered by you.
But in the photograph, of course,
There is no sign of this tragedy—
Just you two holding hands,
While your parents sit, lovingly,
On the edge of the diving board.
And that makes you wonder:
Who took this particular picture?
Any clue you hoped to find written
On the back of the snapshot
Has disappeared across the wet surface
And become, more or less, illegible.
This bothers you for a brief moment
Until you wash a week's worth of dishes
And place the photograph in the freezer, again.

So Much Like Marie

So much like Marie—
That's how I saw you:
Slender fingers on hips,
Waiting for the crosstown bus
Which never arrived to claim you
On the first day of winter,
When I thought, surely,
I must have lost my mind.

And there you stood,
Portrait of a girl
Caught in confusion's midst;
How were you to learn—
How could you possibly tell—
That what I chanced upon
Kept the cold lie alive
Another season.

Soon, I followed you down
A strangely familiar block
Where we set up house
On a lot so vacant,
It had no address
And mail failed to find us.

I don't remember the moment
You began to resemble yourself
And slowly grow into the woman
I refused night after night;
I think I loved you best
When you were anyone,
A prism in my hands—
So much like Marie.

What I Could Have Been

I could have been the son you wanted,
The baby asleep in the bassinet,
The freckled faced kid next door,
The boy with the letter on his sweater.

I could have been the young man
You read about in Business Week,
You know, the one who overcame all odds
To strike it filthy rich.

I could have been your guy,
Faithful through the passing years,
Sending you a dozen roses each Monday—
For nothing in particular.

I could have been your father,
Your friend's overprotective pop,
Your mother's favorite brother,
Or an uncle to your cousin Freddie.

I could have been a translator—
Fluent enough to speak ten languages,
And carry an extra tongue or two,
So I would never be misunderstood.

I could have been what I wasn't,
And then a little bit more—
Just so no one really thought
I didn't have it in me.

And I could have been an angel,
Floating on eternity's edge,
Waiting to earn my wings,
Free to try anything I pleased.

Forgiveness

She knows now,
Yet never lets on.
The briefly mentioned name
Rings like any other:
Two syllables lightly pronounced,
An iamb of decency
Fills the friendly kitchen
Where we speak through morning tea.

At another time—
In this same place—
The voices of distant wolves
Were the only company
We kept for years.
And then the irremediable silence,
So stuffed with suffering,
We thought we'd lost it all
And begged to die
Before the next night fell.

The long trail to forgiveness
Sweeps behind the house we share
And runs along a rocky creek,
Where water gently flows
When rain collects there.
Here, we beat yesterday's clothes
Against the smooth gray stones
And slowly watch old stains
Drain below the surface.

The Chief

The chief hasn't been laid
In well over a year.
He'd like to meet for a drink
To discuss this important matter.
He feels he can't tell
Another soul about his problem;
After all, he is the chief
And he doesn't really think
He ought to go around
Pleading for a piece of tail.
He stops short of claiming
It should be his given right,
But I know him quite well—
And that's exactly what he thinks.

The chief wants me to assure him
This won't go any further
Than the two of us.
The poor guy's desperate.
Hell, he's had hundreds of women—
Sometimes, three in a single day;
What's happened to him now? he wonders.
Have I noticed anything unusual
About his demeanor or actions
Which would deter the women
From finding him attractive?
He encourages me to smell his breath
And I must admit it's rather pleasant.

The chief eagerly asks
If there are any available women
I might set him up with
For an evening this week.
Somehow he thinks I have
A pipeline to easy street.
He appears crestfallen
When I tell him I know
No one who would be right
For someone of his position.
Then he lowers his head in shame
And mutters he'd gladly
Wear some type of disguise
Or carry on this little tryst
In another town far away,
Where he's a complete stranger.

In the end, the chief departs—
No better off for having met me.
I agree to make various inquiries
But he seems a beaten man,
Ordering one too many gin and tonics,
Stumbling out of the bar,
Refusing help to reach home.
And I feel like a failure,
Unable to provide him
The most basic of needs,
So when I dream that night
It's the chief's face I see,
Sadly staring down at me
From some distant star.

Five Blind Boys

Five blind boys
From Birmingham's back roads
Appeared before St. Peter
At the midnight hour,
After a terrible crash
Sent them, one by one,
To the gates of heaven.

And why should I let you in?
Peter questioned blind boy #1,
Perturbed to be summoned so late.
Hell, I've been blind since birth—
Ain't that reason enough?
Peter thought for a moment,
And jotted a note to himself.

What about you #2? Peter asked.
What is it you expect me to do?
My sweet momma won't sleep a wink
Until she knows I made it
Inside the kingdom of God.
That so, is it? Peter mused,
And arched his back like a cat.

#3, you know better than to drive
A car at night without a license.
Yes sir, indeed I do,
And I have learned my lesson;
It will not happen again.
Kids these days, Peter quipped.
Then he lit a menthol cigarette.

What's your sad tale, #4? Peter wondered.
Well, it's kind of like this.
I was home alone with the good book
When these strangers broke in
And forced me to commit this sin.
As God is your witness, Peter muttered,
Removing a cloud from his shoe.

#5, I'm a very busy man.
Let's wrap this up, Peter pleaded.
He don't speak, said #1.
Never a word, said #2.
Mute as a stone, said #3.
Ain't it a shame, said #4.
Wouldn't you know, Peter sighed.

St. Peter sent the blind boys away,
Figuring damnation was best left to liars.
He sent God an urgent message—
Something about needing a vacation.
Then he rented one of those
Fancy new sport utility vehicles
And drove like hell through Alabama.

Dream House

I built my dream house
Without windows or doors—
Ceilings or floors—
And no room, at all,
For even a single wall.
I fell in love with the place
Long before I realized
I'd never need a key
To enter or exit.
Friends began to wonder
Where I actually lived;
But I didn't care to share
The address with a soul.
Besides, if they chose
To stop by and visit,
Where would they sit
Or stand, for that matter?
Really, it was just me
And the wide-open space
Money could not provide.
At no time did I mind
The fact that my neighbors
Watched each move I made
Inside my little shelter,
For it was quite clear
I had nothing to hide.
I must admit, I wish
Such bliss, as this,
Had found me earlier.
If I could only manage it,
I'd never leave the house
And spend my entire life
Under a cover of stars—
Asleep on a bed of truth.

Winter's Night

In any other light
I could see the bright smile
And watch your lips twitch
Before they stretch into a grin.
But under the dark glow
Which shadows the candle's flame,
There is more than a hint of sadness
That traps your pretty face
In another place far from where
We lay this winter's night.

I can't tell exactly what it is
I've done to cause such strain
And yet I feel in my bones
I've broken something between us:
Said one too many words
When they were uncalled for;
Taken my two large hands
And touched you where I shouldn't;
Cut the last remaining chord
Connecting us to each other.

What I really know about love
Could never amount to much.
Still, with you I learned
How to gauge the safe distance
A man measures when approaching
A woman like you.
Now, the question of space
Becomes another matter entirely.
Here, beside me you sleep
In a constant state of vacancy,
From which I don't think
You'll awaken any time soon.
And I wrap myself tighter in January—
If only to blanket the gloom.

Chemistry Experiment

We listened intently to the professor,
Followed each one of her instructions,
Read through the textbook twice,
Wore lab coats and safety goggles,
Mixed the perfect chemical combinations
In the proper amounts and order.
It was all progressing smoothly;
We thought we were a complete success.
And then the flash of light,
The loud, perplexing explosion,
The black rope of smoke,
Rising freely above our singed hair.
Someone in another lab down the hallway
Phoned the local fire department
Which arrived lickety-split
With the hazardous waste crew,
And they assessed the accident,
Deciding we were out of danger.
It was the talk of the campus
For many weeks afterwards.
We, however, became so disillusioned
That we immediately dropped the course
And slowly retreated from each other.
The very idea we could have done
More damage than we actually did—
Blown up ourselves and the building
From the base of its foundation—
Shook us, like nothing had before.
And even now, years later,
When anyone still asks about you,
I get this sick feeling in my stomach
And wonder what really happened
To all that elementary matter.

Revelations

You don't know how—
It's never been explained;
There's a process here, somewhere,
But it would probably take
Page after dusty page
From the Book of Revelations
And a century's passage
To teach it to you now.

Still, you ask the man on the street
Where he learned his trade—
Was there a step he took—
A pattern or plan he made—
Or did it all simply
Fall into place when he ate
An orange on a hot day
And saw the sun turn blue.

Thoughts and more thoughts
Continue to plague you.
You find it difficult to sleep,
Fearing the moon will reach down
And grab you by the lapel,
Begging you to tell her
What the hell is the story
And why don't you write it out?

You believe life may end
In the company of misfits,
Men much like yourself,
Who will take their last breath
When air becomes a saleable item;
By then, any lesson gained
Arrives moments too late—
Death, a welcome smile.

The Good Life

It was a mysterious message
I received on my computer screen;
Could she meet me on the Strip?
We had a lot to discuss.
I had no idea who she was.
I didn't respond for a month
But the messages continued daily.
She said I wouldn't regret it
And claimed to be a real peach.
Finally, I concede, I was intrigued—
We met at the Blow Torch on Sunset.

She told me I'd better relax;
It was going to be a long evening.
Out of a black leather bag
Dropped the three books I'd written.
Now the trouble began.
She cited page after page—
Black and white testimony
To indict a lonely life like mine.
I wanted to object, of course,
But found no grounds for any appeal.
A lawyer couldn't have presented
Such an open and shut case.
I was a bit bewildered by it all.
What did the girl want with me?

She ordered a few drinks for us.
I told the crabby bartender
He ought to make mine a double;
She said that was a good idea
And I was more fun than she thought.
Soon I found myself falling for her.
Then she suddenly lowered the boom.
She had no interest in me, whatsoever;
It was all part of a clever ruse.
She actually had a good friend

With a past similar to mine
And felt we were soulmates—
Perfectly matched, but damaged bookends;
Neither of us had a shred of dignity.
She promised we'd be happy together.

I almost fell off the barstool
And yet the proposal appealed to me,
Especially after another martini.
Who in the world was I kidding?
I wasn't getting any younger.
And when a provocative snapshot
Appeared on the counter of the bar
I knew I had nothing to lose.
In short, I told my matchmaking friend
To arrange a clandestine meeting—
Just as soon as possible—
And went to visit the whizbang room.

When I returned to the bar,
I couldn't believe my eyes;
There she sat waiting for me,
Even prettier than her picture.
Her friend had conveniently vanished
And I was filled with questions.
She put her finger to my lips,
Magically produced my car keys
And told me she would take me home,
Because I was in no shape to drive.
On the ride back, I must admit,
I marveled at her manual dexterity—
How she deftly shifted each gear
And handled the tight hairpin curves.

When we arrived at my dark house,
She walked me to the front door,
Reached into her back pocket,
Withdrew another key I'd never seen
And let us in with a shy grin.
Despite the absence of light
She helped me out of my clothes,
Led me ever so gently to bed,
Uttered the 23rd psalm
And then slid in beside me.

From that wonderful night on,
We've never spent a day apart.
What more is there to say
When you've found an angel
Who quotes Keats and Yeats,
While watching the Yankees
Wrap up another World Series.
And yes, I'm a lucky man,
Blessed from head to toe,
Smart enough now to know
How good my life has been.

So What

So what if I never
Lived on the right
Side of the tracks where
Trains ran night and day.

So what if I never
Attended the college of my
Choice and spent high school
Stoned inside my brain.

So what if I never
Fulfilled my dead parents'
Dream and left them
Holding an empty bag.

So what if I never
Climbed the corporate ladder and
Stuffed my jeans with the
Sweet green of success.

So what if I never
Learned to love another
Soul and crack open
Misery's thick black shell.

So what if I never
Took a wife and played
Risk on the happy
Street where you live.

Undone

We are undone.
In the time it takes
For summer to come
And unwrap the spring—
We are undone.
When the sun sets
Upon the green ocean
And day is no more—
We are undone.
By the edge of night,
Beside the bunk beds
Where our children sleep—
We are undone.
On every stranger's tongue
That speaks to us through
A circle of broken dreams—
We are undone.
And at love's front door,
With only a tiny drum
To keep our beat steady—
We are undone.

Your Father's Ghost

I tried—really I did—
To crawl into your life
And make sense of madness
I was unable to comprehend.
Through the small Southwestern towns,
Across the great state of Texas,
I chased your father's ghost,
Never very far behind.
Traveling east on Interstate 10—
Driving home to Lafayette—
I asked him why ... why ... why ...
But he refused to answer;
His lips, twisted and fixed
On the asphalt ahead of him,
Counting each mile as if it were
The last step towards execution.
And I can well imagine—
His soberest day came
When they took you away
And gave you another man's name.
He must have been dead, then,
Before the ink dried on the document,
Yet he would have five long years
To test the depth of his sorrow
At the bottom of a bottle.
As for you, sweet girl,
The past is often unkind
To an innocent child
Along for the ride.

This Case For You

I watch the way you sway
Into the office we share,
Monday, Wednesday and Friday,
Dropping papers, books and exams
Upon the allotted space
I've cleaned for you
Across my empty desk.
You're sighing, yet again,
About the latest tiff,
Telling me, perhaps, it's more—
Some dark funnel cloud
Before the next storm.
You wonder how long
You'll stay with him.

We speak for five minutes
And you dash off to class,
A lecture to deliver on Pynchon.
I hold the novel you gave me—
His first, just to begin—
And smooth out the torn cover.
I finished reading the book
Over winter vacation,
But don't want to part with it,
Especially the passages you underlined
When once you were a student.
I think of the past three months
And know I've got it bad . . .
This case for you.

I wait a few more moments
And slip out of the office
To fetch the morning's mail.
I take the only possible route
That leads me to your classroom.
Through the door's glass window
I find you at the lectern—
Hands softly fanning the air,
As if another germinal idea
Landed safely on your shoulder.
The students follow your every move;
Why wouldn't they, I muse.

Chances are you'll be gone
By next semester's end.
Some doctoral program will surely
Snatch you up in no time
And put you to work for them—
With or without the beau
Who claims he'll follow you
As far as the panhandle.
And what, then, of me?
I'll be left to dwell on days,
When what you wore to work
Kept me dreaming at night,
And how your sweet evergreen smell
Clings to the books I love.

U.S.A.

Here, in America,
We never stand on ceremony
But move easily through life,
Taking it all in stride,
One day at a time.
We unfurl the stars and stripes
And elongate the truth—
At all costs—
Because we are free to do so.

Here, in a united America,
We slip into perfect position,
Depending on the issue at hand.
We turn left to center
And center to right—
Sometimes, in the same night,
And strike only when danger
Rears its scaly little head.

Here, in the United Snakes of America,
We slink along on our bellies
And leave each limb to charity;
After all, who needs them?
We detest moral treachery
In the highest office,
Demanding a public execution,
Before we slither off to sleep.

The Plaintive Angel

There is a plaintive angel
Perched upon your shoulder,
Just waiting to teach you
A thing or two about love.
She believes this is the time
You must learn a little lesson
Life instructs those who venture
Off the edge of the precipice
And then try to maintain
Their balance in midair.

Always beware of the descent,
The plaintive angel informs you,
For natural laws are at work
Which you can never prevent—
No matter what precautions you take;
And the plummet to anything earthly
Occurs so swiftly that rock bottom
Is both the first and last jolt
You're likely to feel for years.

You listen to the plaintive angel
And watch how tears collect
In the corners of her eyes.
She has become silent now
And you know the reason why.
At first, the cool, refreshing wind
Dances across your red face
As you drop through space,
But when you glance down,
All you see is the ground
Rising up to meet you.

Timber

The words meant nothing at all;
He scattered them across the page
As if he were feeding chickens,
A handful of grain at a time.
He paused to fiddle with a cuticle
That begged to be clipped—
When had it come to this?

Grunt work, she first called it—
Long before he knew it as such.
You sit your butt down
And spend the entire afternoon;
Sooner or later, something will stick.
Top flight brain surgery, it ain't.
A chapter a month—or else!

Was it ever any different?
Had he always fooled himself?
Even the "serious" stuff
Had a sense of fluff to it—
But it often came down to this:
Where in the world was he?
And where, perchance, were they?

At night, he dreamt about logging;
The giant timber would roll in
And he quickly stacked it
Up to the clear blue sky—
Until he thought his back
Would surely ache and break
From the weight of it all.

Mornings were the loneliest.
He'd tend to what chores he could
And devise a game plan
To make it more bearable;
Then he'd retire to the study,
Remove his socks and shoes
And climb into the wall.

The last time she saw him smile
Was the day of the stroke.
He'd spoken about a vacation
Up in the Northwest territory
Where the chill would slap you silly.
And then he just collapsed—
At his writing desk, no less.

Nursery of Lies

So many hours and days,
So many months and years ...
And it never gets better.
Everything else, they say,
Turns easier with time—
The loss more bearable,
A wound that eventually heals
To leave a flower-like scar,
But not this sorrow
Where grief's garden allows
Only a single weed to grow.

And I have come to know
The uselessness of hope—
How profound despair takes
Even a joyful memory
And slowly chokes it
Until what life remains
Drains into a plot of tears
From which there is no escape.

Empty is the little room
Where you first slept
When I brought you home
And thought about the boy
You could be one day,
Long before a cruel angel
Led you away from me.
Now there is nothing
But space to plant between us—
My weak heart, a wet stone
In this nursery of lies.

Hair Care

I thought about hair
For most of last night
And into the early morning.

I thought about hair color
And why it seemed so limited—
The natural kind, of course.

I thought about hairstyles
I wore many years ago
And what it all meant.

I thought about hairnets
And the women who wore them
In the cafeteria at Teaneck High.

I thought about great hair,
Who was lucky enough to grow it,
And those of us who were hopeless.

I thought about hair care
And all the money to be made—
But I was hampered by poverty.

I thought about hairdressers
And why they give you dirty looks
If you call them that, nowadays.

I thought about haircuts
And how a bad one could ruin
A month of my wife's life.

I thought about hair loss—
Became severely depressed
And stuck a hat on my head.

Only a Game

You said it was only a game
We could try awhile
And see what happened:
No strings, no rules, no paper,
Nothing to tie us together
But pure unadulterated love.
And, yes, I agreed to this.

There was no white picket fence—
Merely a safe place to sleep
And keep the cruel world
From turning upside down.
You had a job; I had none.
Long spaces of time passed
Before I began to see
What an odd life we shared,
And yet I was unable
To roll away from you,
Stuck with the single chore
I assigned myself to do.

I admit I wasn't adept
At cleaning things up.
You were right to call me
The queen of utter clutter,
But you were a neat freak—
So what did that teach us?

I don't know when it ended;
Perhaps it was the day
You threw a dirty shirt
Into a washing machine,
So crowded with clothes,
The door refused to shut.
I guess I realized then
We were on our way out.

Even on a good day
We were a bad match.
Still, I wish you the best;
I just hope you found
The tearful trail I left
On your side of the bed,
Before you fled the home
Where we once played house.

Memorandum

What nature has to offer
I could do well without;
Just stick me in my house
And seal the windows shut.
You can take the sun—
For what it might be worth—
And let it burn down
To nothing but a tiny spark.
Life in the dark
Wouldn't set me back much.

I figure I've seen enough
For three and a half lifetimes;
Whatever hasn't happened yet
Awaits, a twisted snake,
Ready to strike me dead
The second I step outside.
Storms, quakes, drought and frost
Make these poor joints ache
And swell until the pain
Brings a flood of perpetual rain.

Fate has left a long memorandum
Nailed to my front door;
Its words read like a whodunit,
But I'm too lazy to think
And too feeble to turn the pages.
Build me a bed of stones;
Pour me a cup of clay—
One day, this, too, shall be yours.

Bats

You awake in a cave
And find a billion bats
Beating their membranous wings
Above your pretty little head.
How odd, you begin to think,
What are such silly creatures
Doing in this dark place
When they should be free
To fly against the open sky.

And why the eerie red eyes?
Don't the poor, tired darlings
Ever get enough sleep?
No wonder the bats barely see.
A wave of nocturnal admissions
Flutters across your mind,
Faster than you can fear
The fact that a few new friends
Make a nest in your hair
And feel at home there.

But it's how the creatures arrive
That seems to stupefy you;
This super echolocation you read
In some high school textbook
And didn't give a second thought to.
Now you're intrigued and wish
You could speak to every bat—
One mammal to another—
Learning the sonarlike system,
Which would safely steer you
Clear of potential danger
And the unwelcome objects
You bump into each night.

Poetry (In Motion)

A student sitting in my office
Is privy to a conversation
I have with my publisher.
Through a strange quirk of fate
Harley-Davidson offers, possibly,
To ante up bucks for my new book—
Something about improving their image
By taking the literary high road.
"How cool," the young woman coos.
"That's so unbelievably awesome.
Will they put a picture of you
On the back of a bike?"
I tell her quite frankly
This remains to be seen.
We have no sign of money yet—
Only the word of an underling
Who wants a manuscript
Sent to his office,
Somewhere in Illinois,
By this time next week.
"Where the hell is Illinois?"
The inquisitive student wonders.
I think a geography course
With the dynamic Professor Leaver
May do her more good
Than the current poetry class
She visits rather infrequently.
Soon she is on her way,
All filled up by alliteration
And a dash of caesura—for good measure.
I'm left with a curious image of me,
Straddling some red metallic hog,
Dressed from head to toe in black leather,
A rather disconcerting thought.

But, then again,
Things could fare far worse;
I could be perfectly posed
Behind the wheel of my father's Oldsmobile,
Driving the sleek General Motors' dream,
Deep into the new millennium.

Doctors of Letters

Perhaps, she got carried away that day;
Took a step so far inside the box
That she couldn't find her way out—
Rode the kite up so high
She couldn't bear to look down.
No one knows for certain
Why she later became
A name on a police report,
A body for a coroner's inquest,
A poet whose work would always be linked
To the tight noose around her neck.

There are theories discussed
In towers where ivy grows wild;
And Gods speak Greek to students
Who follow them about and hang
On every word that makes the world
A sound and sensible place,
As long as they understand
Madness must be confined to a book
With perfectly numbered pages—
Because that's just the way it is.

When the doctors of letters
Turn back their covers at night
And lay their heads down to rest,
Do they fall asleep any faster,
Knowing how easy it is to master
The art of deception by calling it truth?
And the woman trapped in the sky?
Who listens to her joyful cry
As she drops safely to earth.

The Locomotive to Hell

It's never easy thinking back
To whatever it was you
Wish you had become—
Everything you left behind
While traveling the line,
Measuring each crooked mile.

Often, you wonder aloud
If fate's just a lonely passenger
On a crowded runaway train,
With only a pocketful of spare change
To pay the discount ticket
For a fare that expired yesterday.

And the ultimate shadow
Which habitually tracks you
Hides around the bend,
Impatiently awaiting a sign
From that demon . . . time,
Who rides each shiny rail
Aboard the locomotive to hell.

Dangerous Curve

Just up ahead,
Slightly around the bend,
The road dips down
A country two-lane blacktop
And there she stands
Under the summer moon,
Staring at the sky,
Swimming with silver stars.
She sways to the sound
The wind makes as it slaps
The corn back and forth
Across the open field—
Body in motion,
Heart at rest.
She knows she must leave
This place where nothing grows
Inside her tiny heart
But a dry stalk of grief
She snaps day after day,
Praying for another soul
To share her desolation—
If only for the moment it takes
Until the approaching car
Flashes its high beams
And hurtles to meet her.

Obituary

You sit on a cement wall,
Thinking of all the places
You've never been in the world—
How they forgot to give you
A middle name at birth—
When nothing but blank space
Separated first from last.
Later, in a moment of fatigue,
You stumble upon yourself and wonder:
What's a life worth, anyway?

You figure one day you'll marry—
Only misfits don't find mates—
And take a suitable job
In some metropolitan city,
Where you hope to raise children
And be done with it
By the age of 50. . .
Really, what more is there?

The rope of cigarette smoke
Lifts slowly above your head,
Ringing in this New Year's Eve,
Like those in the past—
Igniting a frightening dilemma
For what's yet to come.

One morning you wake up dead
And return to bed with the newspaper,
Skimming through the obituary page
To learn there is no mention of you.

A ghost arrives at your front door;
He looks you over, laughs and leaves.

Love Story

He told her she was a jewel,
How he worshipped her constantly,
And just to prove it
He offered her anything;
She gazed longingly up at him
And chose his opalescent eyes.
He didn't hesitate a moment—
And gift wrapped them for her.

They grew closer together.
Life was, indeed, splendid.
She taught him to view the world
Differently than he had before.
He was so terribly grateful
That he often wondered
What else he could do for her—
She asked might she have his ears.
He sent them to her the next morning.

It was decided they would marry.
She desired a church wedding,
A choir to sing in Latin
And bells to ring at noon;
He heard only angels in his head.
On their wedding night she explained,
Now that they were truly one,
Could she, please, borrow his voice.
He placed it in a cup by the bed,
Fell soundly to sleep in her arms
And never spoke a word again.

Unquestionably happy were they—
Year after year after year—
With children and grandchildren
To keep them busy and fit
Through each of the seasons;
But if the truth be known,
He always felt a bit guilty
About that first day they met,
When he sat in the park
And devised his wicked plan
To steal her tender heart.

The Cost of Being Me

The cost of being me
Arrived in the mail
Late last night before
I crept slowly to bed.
I read the expenses
And thought them through.
They were perfectly itemized,
Line by individual line.

My parents charged me
For being a rotten kid,
Becoming a general nuisance,
Having another mouth to feed,
Incurring the cost of clothes,
And providing for my wayward education.
This, more or less, said it all.

The price of companionship
Also appeared quite steep.
Close friends demanded payment
For their precious time
And dutifully listed at least
A hundred different complaints—
One indiscretion after another,
Concerning my disloyal treatment
Over the past five decades.

With colleagues from work
I'm afraid I fared no better;
They claimed my job performance
Left much to be desired
And exacted immediate compensation
For covering my sorry ass
On so many occasions,
They'd lost any accurate count.

As for my former wife,
Well, what shall I cite?
That I was an unfaithful mate?
That I squandered our fortune
On a pony or two or three?
That she took my good name
Before I brought it to a bad end?
That I once challenged my mother-in-law
To a wrestling match on the porch
In front of the neighbors?

But it was certainly the children
Who informed me how penniless I would be.
The extreme pain and suffering
Of having me as their dad
Had crippled them clinically
Beyond what any therapist
Could reasonably do for them.
My kids were scarred for life
By a general inability
To cope with any form of reality
And had to be duly recompensed
For the rest of their days.

I've totaled it now
And find just how fair
It all appears to be.
I'm really quite amenable
To the cost of being me
And don't plan to put up
Any defense on my account.
There's little to quibble with,
Except for the dog's accusations . . .
But that's entirely another matter.

It was the one season
He'd dreamed of his entire life,
An eternal summer when the ball
Floated towards home plate
As big as a grapefruit.
He squarely planted his feet,
Pointed his bat skyward
And waited for the chance
To launch another long drive
Beyond the outfield fence,
Where fans gathered to catch
History in their hands.

The pitcher's deliberate pace
Did nothing to unnerve him;
He knew the routine by now—
How not even a patron saint
Wanted his name left to rot
In the sacred record book
For future generations to read,
As the poor, unfortunate soul
Who made this moment possible.

He stepped out of the box,
Knocked some dirt from his spikes,
Adjusted the cap that bore
The name of the city he loved
And heard his father's voice,
Coaxing him to relax,
Take a deep breath:
Remember, this is just a game
Children play for fun.

And then came the wind-up...
One arm twisting overhead,
The release which sent the sphere
Rapidly spinning for home.
Later, he swore he saw
Each minute revolution
Before the crack of bat to ball—
And the great row of faces,
Straining to follow the flight
One man made in early October,
On a hazy Sunday afternoon,
When he dared to chase
Time and alter space.

—for Mark McGwire

Losing Olivia

You could have told me
I wasn't the one for you;
It would have saved time
And a lesson in grief
I learned far too late.

You could have told me
We really had no chance,
For I was clueless—
Odd as it may seem—
I'm a bit foolish that way.

You could have told me
Just how silly I appeared,
Trailing after you each night,
A chrysanthemum in my hand—
This stupid song on my lips.

You could have told me
What happens to poor souls
Who leave their hearts out
Too long in the rain,
And fail to find them again.

You could have told me
Love is a fickle thing
I had no right believing in;
That's what I wish you said:
But Liv, you never did.

Reaching for Heaven

You tell those ugly lies—
Big, juicy ones to convince me
That truth is nothing
You'd wish upon a fool.

I wonder why you say such things.
I'd like to open your brain,
Just to see what's there;
Yet I'd be deathly afraid
To put it back together again.

Listen to me for once:
It can't go on like this.
I've half a mind to pack my stuff,
Leave this dumb letter
And be done with you forever.

I picture you reading my scrawl
In an empty, windowless room—
Grinning, as you sit by candlelight,
Puffing on a Cuban cigar,
Smoke slowly escaping your lips.

You say there is surely
No greater curse than the love
We commit to each other—
How only deranged angels
Ask to sing in choirs
For which there is no asylum.

I've had one more sherry
Than you tell me I should.
The moon hangs precariously,
Dangling by a single thread;
But I'm far too tired
To reach for heaven.

Dwiggins

Dwiggins dreamt that wild dogs
Chased him endlessly
Through the streets of Fort Dodge,
Their tongues hanging down
From their frothy mouths,
Hoping for nothing less
Than a fresh taste of flesh.

Dwiggins couldn't justify
What he'd done to deserve
Such a terrible fate.
Had he ignored a stranger?
Deceived the elderly pastor?
Wished for something he shouldn't?

For a man who always slept soundly,
Poor Dwiggins remained distressed—
Especially when the disturbing vision
Returned to hound him
Night after frightful night.
All right, he finally thought.
Enough is enough.
I'll stop these monsters
Dead in their tracks.

When the next evening arrived,
Dwiggins devised a dastardly plan;
He slowly dressed for bed
In nothing but his own skin
And waited, with one eye open,
Until the clock struck revenge—
And he heard the familiar pack,
Baying beneath his window,
As if he, alone, possessed
The only bone in town.

Dwiggins unlocked the front door
And invited the mongrel throng inside.
Their luminescent green eyes dispensed
A weird glow he'd never seen,
But he offered them supper
And bid them all to drink
From the benevolent cup
He held in his right hand.

Bloated and sated by esculent sin,
The creatures collapsed in a circle
And soon began to snore
On the living room floor.
Dwiggins glanced at the drowsy beasts
And the carving knife
That lay across the kitchen table.
Then he trundled off to bed
And slept for six days straight.

Last Request

Just one last request—
It's all I ask—
A small act of kindness
I wish to remember you by,
When winter slips into spring
And we stand no more,
Huddled against the stiff wind
This time of year brings.

Please don't let them know
How it was we came
To love each other;
Why yours were the arms
I chose to wrap around me—
A shawl of forgiveness
I wore to face the cold.

And don't tell woeful tales
That trap the truth in lies,
Where body and soul collide
Under the sad guise of reason.
Step gently away from temptation—
The profane urge to shed
What little remains of our skin.

About the Author

Bart Edelman was born in Paterson, New Jersey, in 1951, and spent his childhood in Teaneck. He received his undergraduate and graduate degrees from Hofstra University. He is currently professor of English at Glendale College, where he edits *Eclipse*, a literary journal. He was awarded grants and fellowships from the United States Department of Education, the University of Southern California and the L.B.J. School of Public Affairs at the University of Texas at Austin, conducting literary research in India, Egypt, Nigeria and Poland. His poetry has appeared in newspapers, journals, textbooks and anthologies, and he teaches poetry workshops across the United States. Collections of his work include *Crossing the Hackensack* (1993), *Under Damaris' Dress* (1996) and *The Alphabet of Love* (1999). He lives in Pasadena, California.